21 Poems From 2021

Antonia Perry

BookLeaf
Publishing

India | USA | UK

Presentation by *BookLeaf Publishing*

Web: www.bookleafpub.com

E-mail: info@bookleafpub.com

ISBN: 9789357443944

First edition 2022

DEDICATION

Of course, my book is dedicated to my beautiful Daughter Iris Elizabeth, she brightens the darkest of days. It's also for Barkley, who is a better person than I am, despite being a dog.

Iris's Poem

Dada's Girl,
Of her, he thinks the world,
She's his little mini me,
With big eyes inherited from Granna Leigh,
She's a cute little button nose,
But awfully stinky toes,
Scruffy golden blonde hair,
Like her favourite Ted Ted bear,
She's a pixie crop hairstyle,
And the world's most beautiful smile,
She's quite a cheeky cat,
Who's already giving back-chat,
She's funny like Nanna G,
But that could also come from me,
She's short with little arms,
And full of wicked charms,
Impossible not to fall in love,
Because she's sent from heaven above.

Barkley's Poem

Mama's Boy,
Quiet when he has his toy,
Although he sometimes barks quite loud,
He's so gentle he makes me proud,
Especially when Iris is around,
But he never smiles, always a frown.
He's got big brown eyes,
And a terrible stink you can't disguise,
Short legs and four big paws,
He always has a rough dry nose.
He's mainly white with patches of tan,
He's quite rotund, our little man,
He walks with a mincing waddle,
Sometimes likes to sniff and dawdle.
He's a wagging tail and stinky ears,
He loves the froth of Grandad's beer,
Impossible not to fall in love,
Amongst all other dogs, he's a cut above.

Ted Ted

Ted Ted,
Sits on your bed,
Looking soft and fluffy,
And a little bit scruffy,
From the dinner you've shared,
With chocolate round his face,
He looks quite the disgrace,
But you would never care,
Because he's your favourite bear,
Ted Ted.

Grandma's Original Boo Song

Iris Boo,
Did a poo,
In her shoes,
And she didn't know WHAAAT to do.

Iris Boo,
Did a poo,
In her shoes,
And she didn't know WHAAAT to do.

Iris Boo,
Did a poo,
In her shoes,
And she didn't know WHAAAT to do.

The Boo Song

Iris Boo,
Did a poo,
In her shoes,
And she didn't know WHAAAT to do.

Iris Boo,
Mama loves you,
And Barkley too,
So much, so doesn't know WHAAAT to do.

Iris Boo,
Stepped in goo,
On her shoes,
And she didn't know WHAAAT to do.

Iris Boo,
And Barkley Boo,
Mama loves you,
With her heart THROUGH and THROUGH.

Mama Bear and Baby Bear

Mama Bear and Baby Bear
Sat cuddled up one day,
Baby Bear asked Mana Bear
If she would like to play?
'Of course, my dear'
She replied with cheer,
'With you, I could play all day.'
Baby Bear and Mama Bear
Played games for hours long,
Because Mama's love for Baby Bear
Was super-duper strong.

Mama Bear and Baby Bear
Felt tired and ready for bed,
Mama Bear told Baby Bear
It was time to rest their heads.
Both happy inside from the day they had shared,
It was easy to see how much Mama cared,
She kissed baby goodnight,
Wished her sweet dreams,
And told her 'Sleep tight,'
Excited to see her again in the morning.

Iris's Limerick

There once was a girl called Iris,
Born in the middle of a virus,
She let nothing stop her,
Not even a cougher,
She's stronger than the dreaded Osiris.

Barkley's Limerick

8

There once was a Bulldog called Barkley,
When he slept he snored quite sharply,
He dreamt about bones,
And all the toys that he owns,
Not one of them is clean or sparkly.

A Little Girl and Her Bulldog

There once was a girl and her Bulldog,
Together they lived in a bog,
Both covered in mud,
And all kinds of crud,
They were dirtier than a hog.

My Perfect Iris Flower

You are my perfect little flower,
Most beautiful and full of grace,
Your beauty fills my heart,
When I look upon your face,
Mamma loves her little girl,
To me you are the world.

Spring's Beauty

After every storm that passes,
I see a happy cloud,
Because his friend the rainbow's near,
Standing super-duper proud,
Together they water the flowers,
And create a spectrum of beauty,
Some are soft and delicate,
Others striking or fruity.
In your darkest hour,
When the clouds begin to form,
Don't let yourself forget,
Spring's beauty stems from the storm.

Accrington Stanley

It was Iris's first football match,
A win, could Stanley catch?
They played against Plymouth Argyle,
We sneaked her through the big turnstile,
She sat on Mama's chest,
Singing 'Stanley are the best'
She cheered until half time,
The atmosphere was sublime.

Iris clapped along with the fans,
Who stood in the Wham stands,
With every goal that was scored,
The fans of each team roared,
Just one goal Stanley could snatch,
Poor Stanley lost the match,
We still had a brilliant day,
Despite the match not ending our way

Under the Floodlights

Nestled in the bosom of the Northen Hills,
Sleeps a bleak East Lancashire town,
Sprinkled with soot form the forgotten Burnley
Loom,
A change is coming,
The Great Game Football is about to bloom.

On a Baltic winter evening,
The crowd herds out of town,
Winding down the road and under the culvert,
Following the rumble and the road,
They're heading to Jordan North's happy place,
The magnificent Turf Moor.

The floodlights crack through and ice kissed sky,
The fans feel warm and fuzzy in their stomachs,
Some are certain they'll win,
Some pessimistic they'll not,
One thing is for certain,
They'll be in the Miner's supping Bene n' Hot.

Iris Flowers

Iris rainbow flowers,
The most beautiful of all,
Velvety, soft and delicate,
Stems hold their flowers tall,
An array of enchanting colours,
Sway delicately in the breeze,
If you suffer from hay fever,
They'll surely make you sneeze,
They bloom in the springtime,
Returning year after year,
When the buds shoot up,
The bees, they clap and cheer.

The Coppice

Up a long and
Winding Path,
Starting with,
The Steps,
Into a beautiful
Woodland,
Past carved
Wooden Mushrooms,
And a volery of
Birds,
Up to the
Monument,
That looks down over
Accrington,
You can choose from
Several Paths,
There's the steep
Cardiac Hill,
Or you wander to
Arden Hall,
Each of them is
Beautiful,
For I have seen them all.

Tiny Dancer

Iris loves to dance,
The genre doesn't matter,
It's sometimes even trance,
She loves to bounce and swing,
If Bohemian Rapsody is playing,
She even tries to sing,
She can pirouette, dance and twirl,
When she can clap along,
She's a happy little girl.

Brush Your Teeth

Give your teeth a brush,
It's important not to rush,
If there's spots that you miss,
Nobody will want a kiss,
Because your breath will be smelly,
With a stink right down from your belly,
Brush from the front right to the back,
And remove that nasty plaque.

Christening Day

Soft flakes of snow fell,
On your Christening Day,
Everything went swell,
Perfect, some might say.
A spell of childlike purity,
Kissed our little town,
With a blanket of security,
As snowflakes drifted down,
Wrapped in perfect virtue,
Modest, elegant and pure,
For nothing could ever hurt you,
You're protected from heaven forever more.

Night Skies

Did you see
The Man in the Moon?
Look again,
But do it soon,
Before he shy's
Behind a cloud,
Shout 'Hello!'
Shout really loud!

Did you see
The Moon tonight?
A beautiful crescent,
All sparkling and white.
Like the Cheshire
Cat's cheesy grin,
Its beauty puts
My head in a spin.

How beautiful is
The Sky tonight?
With stars that sparkle,
And twinkle bright.
They reflect like
My girl's beautiful eyes,
I dream of her
When I gaze at the skies.

Grandad's Birthday

It was Grandad Neil's birthday,
We all went round to play,
And have a buffet tea,
The room was filled with glee.
Sprinkles topped his birthday cake,
Enjoyed, even by Uncle Jake,
We all sang 'Happy Birthday,'
The full night we did stay.
It was a fun little party,
Quite boisterous and hearty,
Iris helped blow out the candles,
It was a lot for her to handle,
Soon ready for her bed,
Quite stuffed and well fed,
And so, 'Na night' she said
Before she toddled off the bed.

What's a dental therapist?

'I hate the dentist,'
Words I sometimes hear,
'I don't like coming to dentist,'
Often falls upon my ears.
'I am not a dentist!'
I often want to shout,
I am a Dental Therapist,
So, listen, hear me out.
We sometimes work off a referral,
But are clinicians in our own right,
We're passionate about prevention,
To keep your pearly-whites bright.
We'll treat you if you've got gum disease,
And we fill cavities that need filling,
We can extract poorly baby teeth,
And carry out hall crowns with no drilling,
Next time you have a visit remember,
No-one here intends to be scary,
Not even Mr or Mrs Dentist,
Just pretend you're visiting the tooth fairy.

www.ingramcontent.com/pod-product-compliance
Lightning Source LLC
LaVergne TN
LVHW050305200726
843509LV00015B/3168